Brimming with prac
*the Children Worship*
the joy and responsibility of incorporating our children into
corporate worship. I wish I had this book ten years ago!

Brian H. Cosby
Author of *Giving Up Gimmicks: Reclaiming Youth Ministry from an
Entertainment Culture*
Pastor, Wayside Presbyterian Church
Signal Mountain, Tennessee

In *Let the Children Worship*, Jason Helopoulos not only makes
a reasoned and biblical case for including children in worship,
he instills a sense of anticipation of what will happen as
children are not only blessed by their presence among the
body of Christ but also bless us with their presence.

Nancy Guthrie
Bible Teacher and Author of the *Seeing Jesus in the Old Testament*
Bible study series

It has been said that the reason young people are abandoning
church is because their parents never taught them that
church was important. Well, the most obvious way to do
that is to impress upon our children the vital seriousness and
significance of Christian worship – yet many parents, pastors,
and elders feel woefully unprepared for that. Therefore, it is
a pleasure to commend this short book by Jason Helopoulos.
In a series of short chapters, he explains the nature and
importance of worship and then offers practical guidance on
how to communicate this to our young people. This is a very
useful and practical book which deserves to be widely read in
our churches.

Carl R. Trueman
Paul Woolley Professor of Historical Theology and Church History
Westminster Theological Seminary
Philadelphia, Pennsylvania

Addressing little children directly in the course of a regular worship service has become, for me, a much anticipated and rewarding part of reformed, covenantal worship. In Jesus' ministry, the disciples were at one point indignant at the presence of children, as though granting them particular attention seemed beneath the purposes of Christ's mission. They were immediately chastised. And here, in this fine book, Jason Helopoulos makes a compelling Scriptural case for the inclusion of children in worship. It deserves serious and sustained consideration.

Derek W. H. Thomas
Senior Minister, First Presbyterian Church
Columbia, South Carolina
Robert Strong Professor of Systematic and Pastoral Theology
Reformed Theological Seminary, Atlanta, Georgia
Fellow, Ligonier Ministries

Sundays can be the hardest day of the week. I often find myself behind the piano, trying to focus on the tune instead of the visitors I invited for lunch, one eye on my pew-full of children. Jason's book provides solid refreshment for parents and church leaders, encouraging us to think clearly – biblically! – about what worship is and why we do it. Theological framework and practical applications for parents and leaders make this a book useful not only as a how-to guide, but also as a guidepost, encouraging us to view worship as a foretaste of heaven along our earthly pilgrimage.

Rebecca VanDoodewaard
Author of *Your Future 'Other Half'* and *Uprooted*
Grand Rapids, Michigan

# LET THE
# CHILDREN
# WORSHIP

## JASON
## HELOPOULOS

CHRISTIAN
FOCUS

Jason Helopoulos is associate pastor at University Reformed Church in East Lansing, Michigan, and a guest blogger at The Gospel Coalition. He is ordained in the Presbyterian Church in America. He and his wife, Leah, are parents of two young children, Gracen and Ethan.

Copyright © Jason Helopoulos 2016

paperback ISBN 978-1-78191-909-5
epub ISBN 978-1-78191-960-6
mobi ISBN 978-1-78191-961-3

10 9 8 7 6 5 4 3 2 1

Published in 2016
by
Christian Focus Publications, Ltd.
Geanies House, Fearn,
Ross-shire, IV20 1TW, Scotland.
www.christianfocus.com

Cover design
by
Paul Lewis

Printed by
Bell and Bain, Glasgow

# CONTENTS

To my two children, Gracen and Ethan

You are 'my joy and crown' (Phil. 4:1). I continue to pray
that you would know, love, serve, seek, honor, and delight
in the Lord all the days of your life. May you find eternal
and lasting joy in the presence of our Risen King.

# Introduction

Nothing compares to Sunday mornings. We rise early, dress, eat breakfast, and head out the door with Bible in hand. We walk in the front entrance of the church, down the hall, and file into the sanctuary. As we take up our customary seat, other individuals—men, women, and children—begin to stream through the door and take their regular seats. The room fills with familiar people and the love feels almost palpable. You know the scene; it occurs every week. In one sense it is very common. In another sense it is not common at all. As the call to worship sounds, the church gathered stands and with united voice sings beautiful praise to God enthroned above. Thankfully, I pastor a church which loves to sing. The voices fill the room and the sound delights my soul. In that moment, truly heaven and earth meet. The songs we sing rise above the clouds to mix with the anthems sung by angels and church triumphant before the throne of the Lamb. And from heaven, by the Spirit, the grace of God cascades down upon His people as we sing His praise, hear His Word, and pray in faith. Though I have belonged to the church for years, this weekly event continues to give me chills.

During the opening hymn I love to look around the sanctuary. Here stand individuals different in so many ways, yet united as they approach the sovereign Lord of the universe. They journeyed to this church from different walks of life and with different stories. Different ethnicities, races, and colors of skin are observable. Men and women sing together. The old saint in the wheel chair, single young man, the recently widowed mother, the four-year-old child, and the teenager all united in song to God. Blessings flow down, praises go up. Is there a sight on earth more glorious?

As I gaze around the room during this opening song my eyes inevitably land on a child. Few things encourage my soul more than seeing children sing with all their little strength to God. They possess no inhibitions; they were told to sing and so they sing with a full-voice. In those moments, I am reminded of God's faithfulness and care. The gates of hell shall not prevail against the church, He will keep His own, and the covenant community of God continues on. A new generation of worshipers confirms this truth. I need that reminder—it does the soul good.

Yet, the more churches I visit, the less often I witness this scene. The people file in, love still exists, and the singing continues. Different races, ethnicities, and colors of skin remain. Men and women fill the pews. The old saint, single young man, and widowed mother are all present. But something is missing—the next generation.

Children can't be spotted. Why? Families with children attend this local church. In fact, they flock to it. Children are absent because this church considers worship on Sunday mornings an 'adult activity.'

A few years ago, I visited a church with my wife and two children. Friendly faces stationed the church doors and we received a wonderful welcome. As we made our way down the hall and towards the sanctuary, a number of people greeted us. We found ourselves met with friendly faces as ushers handed us the morning's bulletin. Someone volunteered to show our family the way to the children's wing. I declined the offer for a tour but accepted the bulletin. As we sat down in an empty row I read, in bold letters, on the front page, 'Our services are not for children. We strongly encourage you to take your children to age-appropriate Sunday School classes which are available downstairs.' As I read this statement of strong encouragement, I found myself in a state of strong discouragement. I had just finished reading this bold declaration when a pastor of the church ascended the platform, provided a welcome, and offered a few short announcements. The big announcement for this particular Sunday morning was the unveiling of the church's focus for the year—training the congregation in Christian parenting.

I understand it is not easy to bring our children into corporate worship. But worshiping with our covenant children is one of the most significant ways that we parent as Christians. In the pages of this book, I hope to encourage you, the reader, that our covenant children belong in the worship services of the church.

In chapters one and two we will look at the importance of worship in the covenant community and the marks of biblical worship. Some may wish to skip these first two chapters in order to reach the subject of the book—children in worship. As a writer, it seemed necessary to provide the foundation before addressing the arguments and particulars. I think those who take the time to read the first two chapters will find the material in chapters three and four more convincing. Chapters five and six detail practical advice for parents and church leaders for incorporating children into corporate worship. Many of us stand convinced of this needed practice, but long for some encouragement and help in the actual nitty-gritty of implementation. Let's be honest, it is not always easy to have children in the pew. Chapter seven addresses some of the common replacements and objections to including children in corporate worship, while the appendix includes some testimonials and additional resources.

I write this book as a pastor, but even more importantly, as a father of covenant children who has struggled with his children in the pew. Yet, I believe the struggles are worth it, for one of the great benefits our covenant children enjoy is the privilege of attending weekly worship. I am convinced that we neglect this benefit to their harm and our corporate injury. If only one church or even one family worships with their children after reading this book, this author would count every minute of writing well-worth the effort. However, I continue to pray for an even greater work of the Spirit in our generation. I pray the Lord would convince the Church that it should include even its youngest members in worship. What a blessing it would be, if all, or even most of this generation's churches would once again let the children worship! I pray that we might see that day in our time for the sake of our covenant children to the glory of God.

# 1 Why Does the Church Worship?

Last night I sat with my eight-year-old son as we ate a bowl of ice cream together. In between delectable bites he asked, 'Daddy, what is your happiest memory?' I told him a couple of my happiest memories as he attentively listened. I drew out the telling of each memory with details and my son sat enthralled. Both of the stories relayed a time that I felt especially loved. When I finished, he said to me, 'Daddy, I also love being loved. I love that feeling. It makes you happy.' He then asked, 'But do you know what the problem is?' He didn't wait for my answer, quickly responding to his own question, 'The feeling doesn't last long. You feel really happy and loved and then something happens and you don't.' I said, 'That is true, son.' He replied, 'Daddy, heaven won't be like that. We will always feel happy because we will always be loved. It will never stop.' I was a little surprised at my eight-year-old son's deep thought and said, 'That is a really good thought son.' He said, 'Yep, you said that once in a sermon.' Now, I knew that it was a really good thought! A thought he learned by sitting in the pew. As a Christian parent, I pray beyond all else that my children will know the breadth and length and height and depth of the love of Christ that surpasses knowledge, that they might be filled with all the fullness of God forever (Eph. 3:18-19), because that is why they exist.

## THE CRUCIAL ISSUE

What is the crucial issue for our generation? Is it the spread of disease in Africa? Conflict in the Middle East? Terrorism? Or maybe the decline of morality in the western world and the undermining of family structure in our society should receive this designation—divorce is rampant, couples living together before marriage has spiraled out of control, homosexual union has been embraced. These all serve as important issues for our generation, but they do not hold the title of *the* crucial issue.

In fact, *the* crucial issue for our generation remains the same as it was for the generation before us. Yet, not only was it the same crucial issue for that generation, but for the generation that came before it, and the generation that came before it, and the generation that came before it—all the way back to the Garden of Eden. What is *the* crucial issue for every generation? It is always the same: What will mankind worship?

Women and men search high and low to find their purpose in life. Some spend an earthly fortune traveling the world thinking some destination will help them discover their purpose. Others advocate not traveling far at all, but deep within to find purpose—they advocate a kind of inner search, meditation, and extreme introspection. At best, the first is a high-priced vacation and the second is a navel gazing fool's errand. All one needs to do is sit down and read. The Scriptures clearly articulate the purpose for all mankind.

## CREATED FOR WORSHIP

Listening to the Scriptures saves a lot of money and a lot of wasted time. They do not hide man's purpose, they don't obscure it, and they surely don't dismiss it. Your neighbor, your father, your mother, your wife, your co-workers, and your children were created to offer living, conscious, true, faith-filled, passionate, image-bearing worship unto the living God. Every human being who has ever lived was created for this one purpose: to be a worshiper. He gave us breath that we might give Him glory.

In fact, God created all things for His glory. From the grain of sand to the highest mountain, from the inanimate to the living, from massive galaxies to the smallest cell, from angels in heaven to the snake slithering on the ground—all created with the purpose of 'ascribing Him the glory due His name' (Ps. 29:1-2). And in the midst of all the grand scheme of creation, mankind sits center stage. God created mankind alone as His image bearers (Gen. 1:27). Men and women possess the privilege of reflecting His glory in a rather unique and brilliant way that surpasses everything else.

I love how David is caught up with this thought in Psalm 8. He contemplates the greatness of God and says, 'O Lord, our Lord, how majestic is your name in all the earth! You have set your glory above the heavens' (vs. 1). God's glory stretches beyond the heavens, because even the heavens cannot contain it. What a majestic being! So infinite, transcendent, magnificent, grand, and awesome

15

that nothing can confine Him. Nothing compares to Him. Nothing rivals Him.

After contemplating this truth, David exclaims, 'When I look at your heavens, the work of your fingers, the moon and the stars, which you have set in place, what is man that you are mindful of him' (vv. 3-4). What God-fearing person hasn't enjoyed a moment like this? Sitting outside on a dark summer night and looking up at the stars as their twinkling light fills the sky; you are struck by the realization that you are not quite as big as you think and God must be a great being. Like David, we are amazed that God created all things, set the stars in place, the heavens cannot contain His glory, yet, 'He is mindful of us?' And then the shocking personal thought runs through our minds, 'He is mindful of me!' This reality rattles the soul with delight. It proves to be one of the great mysteries and blessings of all the universe—God is mindful of us. Mindful to such a degree that He chose mankind to shine forth His majesty and glory in a rather distinct and magnificent way—greater than flowers, trees, animals, stars, the heavens, and even angels.

God commissions Adam and Eve, man alone, in the Garden to 'be fruitful and multiply and fill the earth...' (Gen. 1:28). Why? Because they alone can fill the earth with the very image of God. We occupy the place of honor and privilege amidst all created things. We alone bear the prestige of being the chief mirrors in all of creation. To be as it were, walking, living, breathing, image bearers reflecting back to Him His glory. You and me! He created us for this purpose.

As those bearing His image, all of our life is to be an act of worship. Paul says to the Corinthian church, 'So whether you eat or drink, or whatever you do, do all to the glory of God' (1 Cor. 10:31). Yet, as a result of man's fall in the Garden, when he chose to eat from the fruit of the tree of the knowledge of good and evil, mankind's ability to reflect this glory was disrupted. All mankind fell with Adam in that first sin and God's image was marred in us. Now, all people are born into this life as sinners rather than God-fearing worshipers.

## RECREATED FOR WORSHIP

But God did not leave us destitute in our sinful estate. He would not allow sin to possess the final word. Rather, He sent forth His only beloved Son (John 3:16), born of the virgin Mary (Matt. 1:18-25), to live a perfect life and die a substitutionary death in order to redeem a people for Himself (1 John 4:8-9).

Why would God do such a thing? We could point to a number of reasons for God's divine act to save His people, but ultimately we must say that He did so for His own glory. 'In love he predestined us for adoption ... through Jesus Christ, according to the purpose of His will, *to the praise of his glorious grace...'* (Eph. 1:5-6). Thus, God not only created us for His glory, but recreates us for His glory. As redeemed people, the Church serves as a worshiping, glory-giving, image-bearing reflector of God's grace in this world. Paul says to the church at Rome, 'I appeal to you therefore, brothers, by the mercies of God, to present your bodies as a living sacrifice, holy and acceptable to God, which is your spiritual worship' (Rom. 12:1). All of life lived unto Him for His praise and glory.

## RESURRECTED UNTO WORSHIP

We could take this a step further and ask, 'What will the Church do in the new heavens and the new earth?

17

What will we be resurrected unto?' And the answer, not surprisingly, is worship. Revelation chapter 19 pictures the angels, twenty-four elders, and the four living creatures worshiping. 'And the twenty-four elders and the four living creatures fell down and worshiped God who was seated on the throne saying, "Amen. Hallelujah!" And from the throne came a voice saying, "Praise our God, all you his servants, you who fear him small and great" ' (vv. 4-5). This command echoes forth and we will respond in kind. 'But the throne of God and of the Lamb will be in it, and his servants will worship him. They will see his face, and his name will be on their foreheads' (Rev. 22:3-4). God not only created and recreated us for worship, but shall resurrect us unto worship as well.

## CORPORATE WORSHIP

Therefore, it should not surprise us when we find from the foot of Mount Sinai to the temple, to the synagogue, to the private dwellings in Acts, that when God's people gather together they do so to worship the true and living God. We are worshipers, so it makes sense that this is what we do when we get together. Worship binds us to one another; this is our reason for being, not only as individuals, but as a body knitted together in the bonds of Christ. In worship we respond, as individuals and a community, to what we value most. We declare with our lips, hearts, and lives that God occupies the place of importance. We pledge our lives, while proclaiming our deepest desire and greatest love. And we fulfill our reason for being.

The writer of Hebrews underscores the importance of this gathering in chapter 10 verse 25 where he commands us not to neglect meeting together (literally, 'do not forsake the assembly of yourselves'). The word for 'meet together,' refers to the formal gathering of God's people for worship. This isn't just a bunch of friends sitting around and talking about the latest chariot races or football games. God's people gather weekly for worship. It is essential that we gather together for worship. Unfortunately, some Christians make the error of advocating that the Christian life can be lived apart from the gathered church and its corporate worship. Whatever the reasoning behind such an argument, the idea is disastrous and unbiblical.

For starters, consider the corporate nature of our faith. We are bound together. We are called the 'flock' of Christ (Luke 12:32; John 10:16; Acts 20:28; 1 Pet. 5:2–3), the 'bride' of Christ (Eph. 5; Rev. 19:7; Rev. 21:2, 9), and are told that we are being built into a 'holy temple' in the Lord (Eph. 2:21). These are all corporate expressions.

The greatest metaphor for the church in the New Testament is the language of the 'body.' We are the body of Christ. Yes, this speaks of our dependence on the head, Christ Jesus, but it also proclaims our dependence on one another. Paul makes this argument in 1 Corinthians 12: 'For just as the body is one and has many members, and all the members of the body, though many, are one body, so it is with Christ' (1 Cor. 12:12). We are 'joined together,' 'growing into a holy temple in the Lord' (Eph. 2:21), and 'are being built together into a dwelling place for God by the Spirit' (Eph. 2:22). Our lives intertwine and inform one another. We are not meant to be alone. When Christians abstain from church, they deprive themselves of all the benefits of the body (1 Cor. 12).

We could say in a very real way that we possess the fullness of the Spirit in all His gifts only when the church meets. Because there, the person with hospitality ably encourages; the individual with the gift of teaching freely exhorts; the sister with the gift of mercy dispenses comfort; and the brother with the gift of faith sets an example. We shape one another to the glory of God as we live a life of worship together. There is no Lone Ranger Christianity. There is not even a Lone Ranger and Tonto Christianity. Every Christian must participate in the communion of the saints. We belong to one another and need one another. It is essential to a life lived in worship.

As Christians, we live life from Lord's Day to Lord's Day, each week we long to 'journey to the house of the Lord', to meet with our God and with His people. This is the assumption found throughout the Old Testament (Exod. 19; Josh.24; Ps. 150) and the New Testament (Acts 2:42; Rom. 12; 1 Cor. 12; Eph. 4) and should be the natural inclination and desire of every regenerate heart.[1]

## CONCLUSION

The people of God worship. How odd it would be to walk into a church, inquire about their worship services, and find out that they don't actually worship together. They mention their preference for watching movies, playing Yahtzee, or eating brunch with one another. If we heard such a thing in a church, we would rightfully assess that this gathering may be a lot of things, but it is no church. Worship marks the identity of the church, because it marks the identity of its people. This is our calling. Created to worship, recreated to worship, and shall be resurrected unto worship for the glory and praise of God.

---

1. Some of this chapter first appeared in an article I co-authored with Kevin DeYoung in the Christian Research Journal entitled, 'Does the Bible Require Christians To Attend Church?'

# 2 What Should Church Worship Look Like?

## WHAT OF WORSHIP?

We saw in chapter one that God created us to worship. But what is worship? Today 'worship' tends to denote singing. However, the word 'worship' in both Hebrew and Greek, the languages in which the Old and New Testaments were respectively written, literally means to bow down. It paints a picture of one bowing down and kissing the hem of the garment of another. It implies a humble encounter. The writers of Scripture routinely used the word 'worship' to describe the gathering together of God's people before God himself (John 4:19-24). Whatever we say about worship, we must recognize that it entails much more than singing. It encompasses everything the Church does when its members gather together in the presence of God.

What defines the essence of our meeting together in worship? The answer to this question shapes everything we do or don't do in worship. The Scriptures clearly note that we give to God in worship. We give Him praise and thanksgiving as we 'enter His gates with thanksgiving and His courts with praise!' (Ps. 100:4). We give by ascribing 'to the Lord the glory due His name' (Ps. 29:2). We are told the angels in heaven engage in this day and night without ceasing as they gather in worship before the throne of God. Their song reverberates through the heavens, 'Holy, holy, holy, is the Lord God Almighty, who was and is and is to come!' (Rev. 4:8). We give to God by offering our lives as a living sacrifice to Him afresh and anew in worship (Rom. 12:1-2.) We give by bringing our tithes and offerings to Him (Lev. 27:30-33; Num. 18:21-28; Acts 4:32-37).

And yet, we know that God is never a debtor. We can never out-give Him. Therefore, we know that in worship we not only give to God, but He also gives to us. We receive His truth as it is read and proclaimed from the Scriptures (2 Tim. 3:16). We would be lost without this light that shines in the midst of our darkness. As we hear this Word and partake of the sacraments He reminds us of His promises and assures us of our salvation. In worship, He bestows upon us His bountiful love, His immeasurable peace, His abundant mercy, His Fatherly care, His wise instruction, and His gentle rebuke. Our cup truly overflows (Ps. 23:5)!

In this way, worship exists as a dialogical drama. He gives and we receive; we give and He receives. Yet, having said all of this, though we receive in worship and though we give in worship, worship does not primarily consist of receiving and giving. Rather, it is about being. The essence of worship is simply and amazingly God's people dwelling with God. We meet with Him—or better said—He meets with us by His Spirit and Word (John 4). Giving and receiving occur in the context of this relationship we enjoy. As the covenant people of God, God binds Himself to us. He is our God and we are His people (Exod. 6:7; Jer. 30:22). In corporate worship we enjoy the benefits of this reality. We look forward to the full realization of this blessing in the new heavens and the new earth. It is there that God chooses to make His dwelling place among us forever (Rev. 21:3). Corporate worship embodies but a small appetizer of the fulfilled promise that awaits us.

## PRIMARY MEANS OF WORSHIP

This truth shapes and directs the 'how' of worship. If worship is primarily about communing with God, then we must seek to commune with Him by His appointed means. These primary means are as the Westminster Shorter Catechism states, 'especially the Word, Sacraments, and Prayer'[1] God appointed these as the necessary elements and we neglect them to our harm, because by them 'Christ communicates to us the benefits of Redemption.'[2]

God exercises His sovereign grace in both saving and sanctifying His people. Man lacks all reason to boast (Eph. 2:9), for God saves and He works in us for His good pleasure (Phil. 2:13). If it is *God* who does these things, then what's *our* part? Our task is to be faithful to those means that God ordains to work through. We plant and water, but always look to God to provide the growth (1 Cor. 3:7).

---

1.   Westminster Shorter Catechism Answer 88.
2.   ibid.

God chooses to work through His Word. It is the seed scattered that produces fruit (Mark 4:1-20). God 'breathed out' this Word and made it 'profitable for teaching, for reproof, for correction, and for training in righteousness' (2 Tim. 3:16). It consists of truth and no error lies within its pages. It is living and active (Heb. 4:12). It never returns void (Isa. 55:11). All other things may pass away, but His Word never fails (Isa. 40:8; Matt. 25:31). These pages declare life, light, truth, and the promise of peace and eternal joy. Therefore, we want our worship services saturated with the Word of God. Like a newborn baby crying out for their mother's sweet comfort, so we long to hear the words of our Heavenly Father. Nothing compares to it. As Terry Johnson has wonderfully said, we want to read the Word, preach the Word, sing the Word, pray the Word, and see the Word (sacraments).[3] Worship without the Word is like an ocean without water, it doesn't exist.

God also ordains prayer as a means of His grace and communion with His people. Maybe nothing is more lacking in church services today than prayer. A well-ordered service contains multiple and various kinds of prayer: a prayer of adoration at the beginning of the service, a prayer of confession soon after, a prayer of intercession for the needs of the church, the lost, government officials, and the world, and a prayer of illumination before the reading of the Word. Each of these various types of prayer serve the congregation well. Prayers of pleading, thanksgiving, and dedication may also appear in corporate worship. Jesus said, 'My

---

3.   Terry Johnson, *Reformed Worship: Worship That Is According to the Scriptures* (Greenville: Reformed Academic Press, 2000), 37-38.

house is to be called a house of prayer' (Matt. 21:13). What a sad commentary it is upon the state of the church when prayer is minimized or even neglected in our worship services.

In addition, God provides the sacraments, baptism and the Lord's Table, as visible signs and seals of His covenant with His people (Gen. 17:10-14; Matt. 28:18; Rom. 4:11; 1 Cor. 11). As such, they are also necessary elements in our worship services (not necessarily weekly, but frequently). Augustine famously referred to the sacraments as, 'the visible Word.' They confirm before our eyes what we hear read and proclaimed from the Scriptures. However, they not only signify the truths of God's Word, but actually seal these truths to our hearts, minds, and souls. For example, when we approach the Lord's Table, it not only signifies Christ's death for sinners and His blood shed for the forgiveness of sins, but that He died for this sinner and by virtue of His blood shed God forgives my sins. God's promises to me are as real as the wine and the bread are to my touch and my taste.

## THE CHARACTERISTICS OF SOUND CORPORATE WORSHIP

### Biblical
'What kind of worship do you have?' That's often the first question someone asks about a church. Usually the 'style' of music is what is foremost in their minds. However, that places the proverbial cart before the horse. It matters very little what the 'style' of worship is, if that worship is not rooted in truth. God reveals Himself to us

25

in the Bible and the Bible reveals to us what God desires from His people. Therefore, faithful churches strive for biblical worship. What does that mean? It means that, not only do they fill their worship services with the Word of God, as mentioned above, but they also seek to adhere to the teaching of the Bible. As Christians, we derive the elements of our worship services from Scripture. We shouldn't design a church service simply to connect with the masses. Rather we focus on what God prescribes.

## Reverent

Biblical worship is also reverential worship. The Bible teaches that the God whom we worship created and sustains all things. Holiness and transcendence mark Him. He is not like us; He is wholly other. When we embark upon worship we enter into the very presence of *this* God. Therefore, worship precludes casualness. If anything consistently jumps off the pages of Scripture, surely it is the reality that meeting with a holy God is anything but casual. When men and women come into His presence, they know it. Moses takes off his shoes (Exod. 3), Israel trembles with fear (Exod. 20), Isaiah quakes (Isa. 6), Job silences his lips (Job 40), John falls down as though dead (Rev. 1). Even the elders and angels, who worship day in and day out before the throne, don't approach God casually in worship (Isa. 6; Rev. 4). Casual worship of the living, true, holy, sovereign God of the universe just doesn't exist! A holy reverence dominates those who encounter God in Scripture.

Yet, reverence easily eludes the worshiper. Maybe we can chalk this up to the mixed feelings most of us possess about the holiness and otherness of God. Sometimes we want to run towards it and sometimes we want to run from it. There is fear and trembling and yet also this delightful pull. Like Isaiah and John, when we see Him as He is, we are forced to reckon with our own creatureliness. Yet, the Christian also feels pulled by His 'otherness.' It moves us with a desire to become more like Him.

Think of Isaiah and John's lives after those biblical encounters. A kind of awe-inspired striving marked their living. A healthy fear drove them to serve Him and lovingly desire to become more like Him. Any illustration pales in comparison, but I think of my grandfather. When I was a child, he was my hero. He was 6'4", possessed a commanding presence, and seemed able to accomplish anything. When I looked at him I knew I was unlike him. He was a mountain of a man with the strength of a dinosaur (or at least that is what my little mind thought). I loved him and yet also feared him. This love, combined with fear, drove me to honor and please him, in a very real and healthy way. When he spoke, I listened. When he held me, I smiled. I also remember wanting to do what all young boys want to do with the male figure in their life, wrestle. However, even on the wrestling mat of the living room floor I felt anxious. He possessed the strength of Superman. I knew he could crush me. We were two completely different beings. There was a reverent fear and a delightful pull in my relationship with him.

Reverent worship is nothing more than giving God due respect, honor, and adoration. We draw near to Him, but near to Him with solemnity and awe. It is fitting and right. Unfortunately, when we think of 'reverence,' cold and stiff formalism often comes to mind, but reverence should never connote such images. In fact, it should

27

suggest the opposite. Reverent worship is God-honoring worship marked by a high-view of God, wedded to a heart overflowing with love and adoration for Him. In truth, reverent worship simply ties the mind and heart together in adoring God.

## Joyful

In worship we commune with Him, hear promises by Him, receive grace from Him, sing songs of praise to Him, offer prayers before Him, and confess our trust in Him. How could we ever truly worship without joy? Especially, when a worshiper understands Ephesians 2:1-3: 'You were dead in the trespasses and sins in which you once walked, following the course of this world, following the prince of the power of the air, the spirit that is now at work in the sons of disobedience--among whom we all once lived in the passions of our flesh, carrying out the desires of the body and the mind, and were by nature children of wrath, like the rest of mankind.'

When we understand what we were and what God is from Ephesians 2:4-7, how can our worship before God not pulsate with joy?

'God being rich in mercy because of the great love with which he loved us, even when we were dead in our trespasses, made us alive together with Christ--by grace you have been saved--and raised us up with him and seated us with him in the heavenly places in Christ Jesus, so that in the coming ages he might show the immeasurable riches of his grace in kindness towards us in Christ Jesus' (Eph. 2:4-7).

When these truths of the Bible resonate in your very soul, joy naturally erupts!

## Edifying

Our worship services serve God *and* one another. Paul says when we sing to God, we also sing to one another. 'Let the Word of Christ dwell in you richly, teaching and admonishing one another in all wisdom, singing psalms and hymns and spiritual songs, with thankfulness in your hearts to God' (Col. 3:16). Our corporate worship services should edify and 'stir up one another to love and good works' (Heb.10:24). Therefore, 'all things should be done decently and in order' (1 Cor. 14:40), so confusion doesn't rule. Where confusion rules, little edification exists. The complex, foreign, and unintelligible have no place in our worship services. In our modern age, we do well to remember our fathers in the faith and the helpful principle they insisted upon of simplicity in worship. This wonderfully safeguards the congregation and promotes edification in its midst.

## Doxological

Worship is primarily about communing with God. When we stand in the presence of God, praise and adoration flow. Doxology (praise to God) fills the biblical scenes in heaven (Isa. 6:3; Rev. 4:11; 5:9-10; 7:12; 15:3-4; 16:5-7; 19:1-8). The previous chapter underscored the truth that God created and recreated us to exist as worshipers. As His people, our earthly and heavenly service consists of worship. Therefore, we rightfully conclude that our worship services must center upon God and giving Him glory. We desire to abandon anything that obscures this. All our worship necessarily points to Him and 'give(s) Him the glory that is due His name' (Ps. 29:2). As Calvin said, 'For ceremonies to be exercises of piety, they ought to lead us straight to Christ' (Inst. 4.10.29). And as we are led straight to Christ, doxology wells up in our hearts, occupies our minds, stirs our souls, and issues forth from our lips.

## CONCLUSION

The Christian swims in the stream of worship—it is our life, our joy, and our pursuit. And corporate worship, gathering together with the covenant people of God, becomes our chief delight in this life. All the people of God from every walk of life, every level of society, every color of skin, every nationality, *and* every age gathering together to commune with Him. Nothing like it on earth exists—nothing as sweet, nothing as good, nothing as life-giving. It belongs to another world—the world to come. In fact, it is a foretaste of that day when the complete and perfect bride shall be united with the beloved Bridegroom to dwell with Him for all eternity without interruption. Oh how wonderful that day shall be. Come quickly, Lord Jesus!

# 3 Let the Children Worship

We are all natural evangelists for our greatest loves. Parents do this by including children in what they themselves love. I sat with a group of fathers and sons last week for our annual sports get-together. The scene in the room represented this reality. A number of the boys wore ball caps symbolizing their allegiance to a particular professional sports team. It would not surprise you to learn most of these boys rooted for the same team as their father. How did this happen? No doubt, they adopted this team as their own because they watched their father root for this team on countless occasions. No one told the fathers to serve as their team's evangelist. They naturally did so. A mother loves art, so she organizes crafts with her young children. A grandmother loves crocheting, so she shows her granddaughter the new stitch she learned. A father loves fishing, so he takes his young son along on fishing trips. I love to cook (and eat), so many evenings you will find my children cooking alongside me. We all naturally serve as evangelists for our greatest loves, by including others in what we most love. I do this, you do this, we all do this.

The Christian loves nothing more than God. Therefore, nothing excites us more than worshiping Him and we rightfully long for others to join us as worshipers of the Triune God. In fact, this shapes and dominates our parenting. We are not just parents, but *Christian* parents. As worship sits center place in our lives, we naturally desire it to take center place in our children's lives. We want them to value it as we do, love it as we do, and long to participate in it each week as we do, because they love the Lord as we do. Our heart's great desire for our children is that they would be His children; worshiping Him with their entire lives. And a significant part of worshiping God in all of life is worshiping Him with the saints in corporate worship.

Therefore, it should not surprise us that in Scripture the covenant people of God include their children in corporate worship. I cannot give a Bible verse as a mandate for this, as there is none, but there are numerous biblical examples and a clear rationale for doing so.

## BIBLICAL EVIDENCE OF INCLUSION IN WORSHIP

The prophet Joel warns the people of God that the Day of the LORD is coming. Judgment will fall upon the land. Yet, in the midst of this message of doom, Joel declares hope still exists. "'Yet even now," declares the LORD, "return to me with all your heart, with fasting, with weeping, and with mourning; and rend your hearts and not your garments"' (Joel 2:12-13). He reassures the people that the LORD, their God, is 'gracious and merciful, slow to anger, and abounding in steadfast love' (Joel 2:13). By doing so, he echoes the very proclamation God utters about Himself when He passed before Moses on Mount Sinai (Exod. 34:6). Joel, in a not so veiled way, reminds the nation of their covenant obligation before God. God gave them His law; they are to be holy even as He is holy (Lev. 20:26). Joel then calls for corporate repentance and worship from the people of God. He charges them, 'Blow the trumpet in Zion; consecrate a fast; call a solemn assembly; gather the people' (Joel 2:15). He calls worshipers out. Blow the trumpet, assemble the people, and worship. Who constitutes a worshiper in this called out assembly? Only elders? Only men? Only adults? Joel commands, 'Consecrate the congregation; assemble the elders; gather the *children, even nursing infants.* Let the bridegroom leave his room, and the bride her chamber' (Joel 2:16). Joel calls all the covenant people of God, including children, even nursing babes, to assemble in worship as the covenant people before their covenant-keeping God.

This example in Joel is not an anomaly in the Scriptures. We see children included in the worship of God time and again. During the observance of Passover, one of the high days of worship under the old covenant, children were obviously present. Moses expects children to observe the rights of Passover and ask questions as they witness this covenantal right. 'And when your *children* say to you, "What do you mean by this service?" you shall say, "It is the sacrifice of the LORD's Passover, for he passed over the houses of the people of Israel in

Egypt, when he struck the Egyptians but spared our houses' (Exod. 12:26-27). We see the same picture in the observance of the Feast of Unleavened Bread (the seven days which follow the Passover). Fathers instruct their children in the midst of this act of worship, 'You shall tell your *son* on that day, "It is because of what the LORD did for me when I came out of Egypt"' (Exod. 13:8).

We find commands related to the inclusion of children in other worship holidays as well. In the celebration of the Feast of Weeks, we find this command to the Israelite nation, 'And you shall rejoice before the LORD your God, you and your *son* and your *daughter*, your male servant and your female servant, the Levite who is within your towns, the sojourner, the *fatherless*, and the widow who are among you, at the place where the LORD your God will choose, to make his name dwell there' (Deut. 16:11). We find the similar inclusion of children in the observance of the Feast of Booths, 'You shall rejoice in your feast, you and your *son* and your *daughter*, your male servant and your female servant, the Levite, the sojourner, the *fatherless*, and the widow who are within your towns. For seven days you shall keep the feast to the LORD your God at the place that the LORD will choose, because the LORD your God will bless you in all your produce and in all the work of your hands, so that you will be *altogether* joyful' (Deut. 16:14-15).

## MAKES A STATEMENT ABOUT CHILDREN AND THE COVENANT

Why do the Scriptures instruct the nation to include children in these worshiping assemblies of God's people? Clearly, because these children exist as part of the covenant community. From the beginning of the people of God, the covenant community consisted of believing adults and their children. Therefore, we find time and again in the pages of Scripture that God works through the institution of the family. God said to Abraham, 'And I will establish my covenant between me and you and your offspring after you throughout their generations for an everlasting covenant, to be God to you and to your offspring after you' (Gen. 17:7). This promise, like a ribbon of hope, weaves its way throughout the Old Testament (Gen. 9:9; 13:15; 17:19; 26:3; 28:13; 35:12; 48:4; Exod. 33:1; Num. 18:19; Deut. 4:37; 10:15; 30:6; 30:19; 2 Sam. 7:12; Isa. 43:5; 59:21; Jer. 30:10; 46:27). By virtue of this fact, children in Israel received the sign and seal of the covenant community (Gen. 17:9-14), partook of the covenant meals, and participated in covenant worship. As members of the covenant community they engaged in the full life of the covenant community.

This doesn't change when one turns to the New Testament. In fact, on the seminal New Covenant day of Pentecost the Scriptures reassert this truth. God pours out the Holy Spirit upon His people and Peter seizes this occasion not to repeal the covenant family aspect of the Covenant of Grace, but rather to emphasize it! Peter proclaims, 'Repent, and let each of you be baptized in the name of Jesus Christ for the forgiveness of your sins; and you shall receive the gift of the Holy Spirit. *For the promise is for you and your children*' (Acts 2:38-39, NASB). If there was ever a time to alter the designation of children as members of the covenant community, surely Pentecost was the moment. Yet, rather than revoking this designation, Peter emphasizes it. Children have always been and always shall be part of the covenant community.

And the central act of the covenant community, whether under the Old Covenant or the New Covenant, is corporate worship. Therefore, we include children, who exist as part of the covenant community, in the central act of that community—corporate worship. One could rightfully suggest that consciously or unconsciously we make a statement about our children's status in the covenant community by the very act of choosing to include or exclude them from corporate worship.

## JESUS' ATTITUDE TOWARD CHILDREN

Jesus debunks the notion that children are less significant than adults in Mark 10. The scene proves poignant. Parents bring their children to Jesus so He might bless them. The disciples find this forwardness brazen and displeasing. They rebuke these foolish adults. Surely, Jesus doesn't have time for children. He must busy Himself with ministering to the more significant people, adults. But the disciples prove to be the fools. Mark says that Jesus was 'indignant.' He wasn't annoyed, he wasn't slightly bothered, he was incensed that the disciples came to such a conclusion and excluded children from His presence and blessing. He demands, 'Let the children come to me; do not hinder them, for to such belongs the kingdom of God'" (Mark 10:14). He then proceeded to take these small children into His arms and bless them. How many children miss blessings due to the well-intentioned, but faulty-thinking of adults? A reader of the New Testament cannot escape noticing that many of Jesus' miracles highlight His care for children (Mark 5:21-43; 9:14-29; Luke 9:37-43; John 4:46-54).

Ng and Thomas rightfully note in *Children in the Worshipping Community*, 'Throughout history the church has tried, often imperfectly, to follow the example of Christ's attitude toward children. The early church opposed abortion and the exposure of unwanted infants. Hospitals, schools, and orphanages developed as the church's means of caring for children. Christian leaders led the fight to protect children from exploitation in the industrial revolution. Obedience to Christ demands a peculiar concern for children among us. It would be ironic indeed if we consider the welfare of children in every area except that most central point in our life—worship."[1]

## CONCLUSION

The covenant community's very identity is wrapped up with worshiping its covenant keeping God. And this community consists of believing adults *and* their children. Therefore, the church lives out its theology when it encourages and even expects its children to participate in this central event. Jesus said, 'Let the children come to me' (Mark 10:14). It would be odd indeed, if we sought to uphold that principle in every respect except the central act of the covenant people of God.

---

1.  David Ng and Virginia Thomas, *Children in the Worshipping Community* (Atlanta: John Knox Press, 1981), 3.

# 4 Blessings and Benefits

We pulled into the driveway exhausted. Sunday is supposed to be a day of rest, but this morning felt like anything but. It was tiring not because of an early start with a meeting before church, the dressing of children, rushing out the door, conversations after the service, or even the disheartening news about a church member's diagnosis. Exhaustion reigned because our two children couldn't sit still or quiet in the worship service. Rather than worship, it felt like we experienced a tour of combat duty without any medals! The hour and a half service could have been four with all the negotiations, warnings, and discipline that were required. The sermon consisted of three points, and maybe between the two of us, my wife and I could recall one of those. Unfortunately, this week was not unique. Hadn't we just performed this 'tour of duty' seven days previously? Hadn't we worked with our children every day since, so this week's worship would be better than last week's catastrophe? Was it all for naught?

Many parents feel this way in the early days of bringing young children into worship. It feels like self-inflicted torture with no end in sight! But as much as it may prove a struggle and even discouraging at times, the effort is well worth it. The blessings and benefits in the long-run will make all the struggle in the short-run fade like the morning mist in the presence of the rising sun. You may not feel like it today, but keep at it. The blessings and benefits yielded are great.

What blessings and benefits eventually flow? Before we detail a few, let's recognize that we often fall into two primary errors when we approach this subject. On the one side, we over-promise the blessings that come with including children in corporate worship. Some proponents of children in worship imply that it serves as a kind of guarantee for the eternal salvation of our children. If only we could bring every child into every service of the church, they would all believe! However, no such promise exists in the Scriptures and plenty of historical evidence contests that claim. The other error equally troubles. On this end of the spectrum, we undersell the blessing of incorporating children in our worship. We treat the practice as something unneeded and unimportant. One may consider it as a nice add-on if possible, but nothing of great significance. The Scriptures and history also counteract this error. God meets with His people gathered together in worship by the Word and His Spirit (John 4). The blessings that flow from this cannot be disregarded or treated as trivial. It is easy to focus upon the struggles and trials of bringing our children into corporate worship and miss the multitude of blessings. The struggles are limited to the morning; the blessings can be eternal.

## PRESENT IN THE MIDST OF THE MEANS OF GRACE

The most important part of a local church's life is corporate worship. It is here that we hear the Word read and preached, join our voices in song, offer united prayer, confess our corporate sin, partake of the Lord's Table, and administer baptism. The summit of the church's life on earth consists of this weekly gathering, because in this weekly worship the LORD meets with His people by Word and Spirit. He ministers to us by these ordinary means of grace (Word, sacraments, and prayer). We must never forget God chooses to work by means—these ordinary means. Churches and parents can chase after the next creative means by which to impact their children, but nothing holds the promise of that which God Himself clearly ordained. These ordinary means of grace prove effectual. When our children attend corporate worship they dwell in the midst of these effectual means of grace. The more we place them in the way of the means of grace, the better the opportunity for their souls to encounter the God of grace. We recognize the benefit of steering our children clear of harmful things— disobedient friends, busy streets, uncovered electrical outlets, and R-rated movies. Why wouldn't we equally desire to steer our children towards beneficial things— the read and preached Word, corporate prayer, and the sacraments? Steering them away from the means of death is good, steering them towards the means of life is even better.

## Hear the Word Preached

God attaches His promises to His Word. As much as we are able, we want to place our children in the way of this ordinary means of grace. The Word does not return void (Isa. 55:11). As we hear it read and preached it works. It is living and active, sharper than any two-edged sword (Heb. 4:12). We want that mighty weapon bearing upon the souls of our children. There is nothing like it. No fairy tale, novel, historical account, biography, or poem rivals it. It alone works faith (Rom. 10:17) and we want our children to hear it proclaimed with power. The proclamation of the Word is distinct in this way. We may discuss the same Word around the dinner table or read it during devotions, but something unique occurs when we hear it preached. The full-force of its authority is on display as we sit under it with mouths closed and ears open. Our desire should be to see our children sit under this Word proclaimed with power by a man after God's own heart; a man who has been called to preach and apply God's Word.

## See the Sacraments

The sacraments represent before our eyes the spiritual truths of the Covenant of Grace. They serve as a kind of picture in which we can see, taste, smell, and feel the realities of God's grace. This is not lost on our children as they see these sacraments practiced and participated in. The children of Israel asked their parents, 'What does this mean?' (Exod. 13:14; Deut. 6:20). And in a similar way our own children will have questions about what they see and hear. We answer by pointing them to a Savior who willingly died for His own. What parent hasn't experienced the blessing of their children asking questions after a service in which the church administers the Lord's Table? 'Why can't I eat the bread?' 'The pastor says those words every time. Why?' Likewise, it is the rare elementary child who has never asked about the significance or purpose of baptism after seeing another child baptized. 'Was I ever baptized?' 'What is he putting on the baby's head?' 'Why?' What opportunities these covenant signs provide for sharing the gospel with our children.

## PARTICIPATE IN PRAYER

Prayer effectually shapes our hearts and aligns them with the very will of God. As our children bow their heads in prayer and listen to the congregational prayer or prayer of confession, they can't help but hear some of the words, inflections, truths, and graces present in these prayers. And how beautiful it is when they begin to join in praying these prayers. One day I took my five-year-old son aside before bedtime and told him that when I am praying for him he should listen to every word and say in his head, 'Amen, Amen, Amen' with everything he agrees to. I noticed the next night that as I prayed, he shook his head up and down as I prayed something that resonated with him. Since then, I notice he often does the same thing in corporate worship. He prays as the pastor prays in the pulpit and agrees where his little mind understands and comprehends.

The more our children dwell in the presence of the means of grace, the more their souls benefit. God promises to work by these means. We don't want to miss any opportunity for their working in the lives of our children.

## PRESENT IN THE MIDST OF THE ENTIRE
## CONGREGATION

Corporate worship is corporate. The entire body gathers together. This reemphasizes the unity God's people possess with one another. It reminds us that we are one people united in our one Lord, one faith, and one baptism (Eph. 4:5). This blesses the entire congregation. The old saint looks around and sees generations that will carry on the faith once he has passed. A teenager, who may struggle to respect his parents, observes venerable and respected men and women in the community who also believe in Christ Jesus. The young child witnesses other adults possessing the same faith and heart for worship that her parents model at home. As the congregation sings, all the voices of the church unite. When God's people read the confession of faith, they confess the same truth united. When God's people hear the public prayers they voice a loud 'Amen' united. How unfortunate it is when the entire congregation should witness and voice this unity and receive encouragement from this fellowship, but our children remain absent. It steals blessing from them and the greater congregation itself.

An event a few weeks ago in our church service reminded me of this benefit. The week before we prayed in our worship service for an eighty-eight-year-old woman, who was by all accounts on her deathbed. Yet, by God's grace, she made an incredible recovery and only one week later she returned to church. I remember looking across the sanctuary and seeing her standing with arms raised, eyes closed, and singing with a full voice to God. Tears came to my eyes; I found myself rejoicing at God's mercy. I wasn't the only one who noticed her presence and recovery. I overheard two moms comparing notes about their children after the service. Both mothers described how their children exclaimed to them during the service what a delight it was to see this dear saint worshiping with such joy a week after praying for her. It impacted these children. Here was Lazarus come back from the grave and worshiping the Risen Lord. And they noticed. Being in the midst of God's people is a good thing for our children.

### PRESENT WITH THEIR PARENTS
Children constantly watch their parents. They learn by observing, judging what their parents deem important, and what gives them delight. Bringing our children into worship affords them the opportunity to observe the importance and delight of corporate worship in the life of their parents. If they aren't in worship, they won't ever see it. In addition, Lord's Day worship, as we have stated before, stands as the most significant hour of every Christian's week. We long to journey to the house of the LORD (Ps. 122:1). How strange then, when only part of the Christian family enjoys this high-point of the week. If there is something a Christian family should do together in the midst of this fallen world, surely it is worship. Nothing is more significant and nothing is more impactful upon our children's lives.

### DEMONSTRATES OUR WEEKLY PRIORITY
The constant routines of our life possess a formative power. As Clifton-Soderstorm and Bjorlin point out, 'Most basically, it is those things we do most regularly and to which we give primacy that powerfully shape who

45

we are and who we become. Whether it is running five miles a day, practicing violin for two hours daily... Setting aside Sunday morning as sacred time for the express purpose of worshiping the triune God is a habit that forms us into people aware of God's sovereignty, grateful of God's grace, and assured of God's provision.'[1] This is not lost on children who attend worship. In fact, it proves formative as the Spirit works and God pours out His grace upon them. Attending weekly worship underscores the importance of worship and the centrality of God week-in and week-out.

## We Pass On the Story

The Scriptures clearly articulate the duty of parents to instruct their children in the things of the Lord. Psalm 78 provides one of the most beautiful statements of this calling. This song recounts the Lord's care for the Israelite nation. The people of Asaph's generation received this testimony of God's work and provision for the covenant people of God. The generation that came before them handed down this important history. In the psalm, Asaph reminds his generation that they cannot hide this story. They must now pass on this glorious truth to their children. Every generation of Christians bears the responsibility of handing down what they have received—this testimony of who God is and what He has done—to the next generation. As I said in another of my books, *A Neglected Grace: Family Worship in the Christian Home*, we stand in a long line going all the way back to

---

1.  Michelle A. Clifton-Soderstorm and David D. Bjorlin, *Incorporating Children in Worship: Mark of the Kingdom* (Eugene: Cascade Books, 2014), 44.

Adam: a line of faithful people who told the redemptive story of Scripture—*the* story of God and His glorious deeds. We tell this story every Lord's Day morning as we gather in worship as the covenant people of God. As our children participate in the service, they hear this story. They can't miss it. At least fifty-two times a year this story tickles their ears and we pray moves their hearts.

### ENGAGES OUR CHILDREN IN THE STORY

Deuteronomy 6 implies that conversation about and participation in the worship of God occupies such a central part of the life of the covenant child that they will ask their parents the meaning behind different aspects of the worship. Moses encourages parents to seize such moments. In fact, Moses obliges parents to teach the truths of God 'diligently to your children' (Deut. 6:7). Surely, we fulfill this responsibility throughout our week and throughout our day. As Moses instructs, you are to 'talk of them when you sit in your house, and when you walk by the way, and when you lie down, and when you rise' (Deut. 6:7). Yet, nothing engages our children more with the redemptive story than their *participation* in the worship of God.

As our children participate in worship, they take part in the practices of the covenant community, which picture the mighty acts of God as He lives in relationship with His covenant people. Bjorlin comments, 'When children learn and live in the story and its rituals, they absorb meaning on the level of identity and character.'[2] As children participate in corporate worship they enter into the great academy of the Christian faith. We teach,

2.   Bjorlin, p.17

instruct, and even form our children into worshipers. Of course, only God can call people to Himself and make hearts of stone into hearts of flesh (Ezek. 36:26), only the Spirit can regenerate an individual (John 3), yet, participating in the worship of God provides a shaping effect. They not only hear about this God, but encounter Him.

## MAKES A STATEMENT TO OUR CHILDREN

When we include children in worship, we relay the truth that they can worship the one true God. Christianity is not an 'adult-only-religion' and worship is not something that only adults are able to do. God calls on *all* people to worship. Though we may not desire to do so, when we exclude children from corporate worship, we are conveying to our children that either they are not an important part of the body of Christ, are unable to worship God, or are not as important as adults in the eyes of God. We offer a loud and undeniable commentary by excluding them from worship. However, if we include them in corporate worship, set our expectations high for their active participation in this worship, and encourage them in it, then our children rightly come to the conclusion that they are a necessary part of the body of Christ, can offer worship to Christ, and are important in the eyes of God.

## THE ENCOURAGEMENT OF CHILDREN

The entire church benefits from children participating in worship. Many times what we count as a distraction actually provides a blessing. At times, children may be loud and need to be taken out of the sanctuary. At other times, the small fuss of a baby or the rustling papers of a toddler help to encourage a congregation. As has been said, 'If there is no crying, your church is dying.' The sound of young children reminds the adults in the covenant community that their lives are united with these covenant children and it remains essential that they pass on the faith to the next generation. Personally, it often encourages me in my church's monthly prayer meetings to hear covenant children pray aloud. How beautiful it is to hear the prayers of children. What a blessing we enjoy when we look around a congregation and see children singing with a full voice. What hope it promises for the church to see teenagers attentively listening to the sermon. What joy stirs in our hearts when we hear a boy down the pew resound with a loud 'Amen' at the end of a corporate prayer. As much as the body of Christ needs the old seasoned saint, it needs the child. It needs to see their faith, their love, and rejoice in their future.

## THE EXAMPLE OF CHILDREN

Finally, children set an example before the covenant community. Adults must not neglect this essential point. When Jesus blesses the children in Mark 10, He says, 'for to such belongs the kingdom of God. Truly, I say to you, whoever does not receive the kingdom of God like a child shall not enter it' (Mark 10:14-15). Many consider children a distraction to our worship of God. In Christ's eyes they are not a distraction, but an example. As adults, we need children constantly before our eyes, because we need to learn from them. If the kingdom of God is made up of children, then adults might learn a thing or two by including them in corporate worship services. The 'body does not consist of one member but of many' (1 Cor. 12:14). The ear needs the eye and the eye needs the hand.

## CONCLUSION

My kids love candy. Surprisingly, I never needed to encourage my children to embrace candy. Vegetables present another story. Yet, my wife and I labor to see our kids eat vegetables daily. Why? We do so, because we know the benefits that flow from eating vegetables. The fiber, vitamins, and nutrients found in vegetables encourage us to 'fight the fight' of getting a little green in their diet. We know the benefits from such a diet could impact their lives for twenty, forty, sixty, or even eighty years. It is worth the struggle. The benefits that can flow from including our children in corporate worship can impact their lives for not just twenty, forty, sixty, or even eighty years, but for all eternity. If green beans and broccoli are worth the struggle, a season or two of difficulty in the pew is more than worth it.

# 5 Wisdom for Parents

Let's face it: bringing our children into corporate worship is not always easy. Squirming kids, rustling papers, the eyes of others, and a host of other problems often accompany children in worship. Unfortunately, some parents identify Sunday mornings with the most difficult part of their week. I understand. As a family, we have lived it. In no way do I want to dismiss the challenge and at times frustration, but I hope you will see the struggle is well worth it. As Christian parents, we desire above all else that our children would know, love, delight in, serve, and honor Christ. The more they encounter Him through the means of grace, the more likely we will witness this blessed outcome. Corporate worship, as we detailed in chapter two, is above all else a meeting with God in the person of Christ by His Word and by the Spirit. Including our children in this weekly encounter can't help but be a good thing for their souls.

Real challenges confront us as we bring our children into corporate worship, but they are not insurmountable. I want to offer some practical and 'Mom-tested' tips as you attempt to do so.

## TREASURE THE LORD'S DAY

God knew our need for rest. In the very act of creation, He ordains one in seven days for rest and worship (Exod. 20:8-11). This day highlights our week. As Christians, we live from Lord's Day to Lord's Day. And the highpoint of the Lord's Day is gathering together with His people to offer holy worship. Help your children by focusing on this moment throughout the week. Talk about Sunday morning worship all week long. Help your children to see that each week begins with this privilege (Acts 20:7; Heb. 10:24-25). And when the day arrives, model excitement about it. If Mom and Dad reluctantly go to church, then the children will reluctantly go as well. If Mom and Dad criticize the preacher, sermon, or others in the church, then the children will most likely criticize as well.

Cultivate a spirit of joy on Sunday mornings in your home. If this is the highlight of our week, then let's act like it. Talk about how wonderful the day promises to be, wake the kids up with excitement, turn on good Christian music for the whole family to listen to, and put a smile on your face. It's o.k. to smile on Sunday mornings!

## PREPARE APPROPRIATELY

Many of our problems on Sunday morning stem from issues before we even arrive at church. Tired children and tired parents create fertile ground for cranky worshipers.

Be boring on Saturday nights. Send your entire family to bed early. Friday nights can be filled with late-night activity, but Saturday nights should routinely be safeguarded. Sleepy heads make for drowsy worshipers. Lay out Sunday morning clothes the night before, so there aren't complications with finding an outfit that fits well, looks right, or is ironed. This is especially helpful with teenage daughters!

On Sunday mornings, wake your family up with plenty of time to spare. Try not to arrive late or even a few minutes before the service. Rushing out the door at home and rushing in the door at church has discombobulated many children and stymied many worshipers.

On the car-ride to church talk about the passage that you will hear preached, sing a hymn together, and converse about the things of God. This helps to prepare the way for worship. If a visiting missionary is scheduled to share or the Lord's Table is going to be observed or any other unique moment is scheduled to occur in the service, take time in the car-ride to discuss it. This sets the mood and helps them understand and appreciate moments in the service. I practice this with my children, who love the personal interaction and it has the added benefit of not only helping them to prepare for worship, but also helps me.

## IMPLEMENT FAMILY WORSHIP AT HOME

A family that worships together at home finds it much easier to worship together in corporate worship.[1] A child

---

1. As mentioned in the previous chapter, you may find helpful suggestions on this subject in *A Neglected Grace: Family Worship in the Christian Home.*

will find it natural to hear and read the Word of God, sing hymns, confess their sins, and pray. It also helps our children learn to sit still, understand the importance of worship, and focus during prayer. For too many children, worship at church seems foreign, because worship at home is absent.

Many churches preach expositional sermons. This means that you know what you will hear read and preached in the week's service—the next passage. Other churches may preach topically but publish in advance the passages on which the preaching will focus. Some families find it helpful to read the upcoming sermon passage during the week. Read and converse about it around the dinner table and during family worship. The children will then possess a familiarity with the text the pastor plans on preaching. This knowledge will give them some things to listen for in the sermon. My son, when five and six years old, always delighted in expressing his 'knowledge' about the Sunday sermon text. He would often lean over during the service with that kind of child 'whisper-scream,' 'I know that story! I know about that!' It delighted this father's heart, as if I didn't know and hadn't led him through it earlier in the week for that very reason.

## START EARLY

Many believe it is more challenging to introduce a three-year-old to corporate worship then a twelve-year-old, but this is simply not true. A three-year-old is in the formative years of training. They are not yet 'set in their ways' and remain quite teachable. They want to please Mom and Dad, though at times it does not seem like it! A twelve-year-old possesses his or her own thoughts on what should be expected and 'endured.' This creates far more challenging issues than wrestling with a three-year-old to sit still. All this to say: it is far easier to begin with small children, so start early. Keep reminding yourself that a few months of struggling with a three or four-year-old teaching them how to sit still in corporate worship yields benefits for the rest of their lives.

Some of us came to this conviction late. Our children may have already reached their teenage years and we regret they weren't in corporate worship with us earlier. If you find yourself in this place, keep reminding your heart and mind that God's grace is sufficient. Do not be 'hard' on yourself. You didn't ruin your children and this doesn't make you a 'bad parent.' Yet, I would remind you, if your children still reside in your home, it is not too late to start. Don't wait. Begin now and seize the years remaining.

## TEACH THE SONGS

Teach young children some of the songs regularly sung in the service. Most children love singing and singing nicely serves as an entry point into their fully engaging in the service. Practice during family worship the Doxology, Gloria Patri, A Mighty Fortress is Our God, or any other hymn, psalm, or song that your church regularly sings in corporate worship. Young children will begin to love these songs and sing with their full-voice when they hear it in church. I preach at one church where a young girl, maybe eight years old, sings with a full-voice every song she knows. Everyone knows when she knows a song! Her voice fills the room and it is always off-key. But each time I hear that little voice a smile creeps across my face, because I have no doubt that a smile occupies the face of our Lord as well.

## USE MOMENTS IN THE SERVICE

Use transitional moments in the service to whisper in your child's ear how much you love a certain verse in a hymn, need to remember to pray for the sick person mentioned, or feel convicted by a certain application. Sometimes I whisper a short question in my child's ear about the sermon—something that will pique their curiosity or help them to listen for an answer. It keeps them engaged and allows them to see you participating intently in the service as well.

## MAKE IT SPECIAL

Make corporate worship something young children look forward to not only for the worship itself, but the time they get to spend with Mom and Dad. Allow the youngest children to sit on your lap in the service. With elementary age children, put an arm around them so they sense your affection. Most young children love these opportunities. Utilize them.

## EMPLOY THE OBVIOUS HELPS

We often forget to employ the helps that already exist. Ask an older child to find the Bible passage or guide your finger over the text for a younger child as it is read in the service. Use the bulletin to show your children at what point you are in the service. If your church uses a hymnal, ask your child to mark the hymn pages that will be sung in the service. As the confession is read, point along with each word and speak so your child can hear you.

## ENLIST THE SUPPORT OF OTHER MEMBERS

Ask another member to lend a helping hand by sitting with your family. Sit beside other families who will encourage you and not fuss if your child turns a little restless. In our early years as parents I often preached every week. Practically, my wife functioned as a single mother most Sunday mornings. Another family in the church came alongside of her and often sat in the same row to help her with two active children. This served as a great encouragement to my wife and to her husband! Don't be too proud to ask for help. Allow others to use their gifts for the glory of Christ and your good. Helping your family during corporate worship may be the highlight of the week for empty-nesters or teenagers in the congregation.

## ENCOURAGE ACTIVE PARTICIPATION

Help your children to participate. Encourage them to pay attention to the sermon, to stand when everyone stands, to sing when the congregation sings, to bow their heads in prayer when the congregation prays, and to give to the offering.

The sermon can be the most difficult time for anyone to stay engaged in the service, let alone a child or teenager. All our minds drift at times. As Billy Graham once said about prayer, so it is true of the service, 'The birds will fly through, just don't let them nest.' Your mind will drift at times, but as soon as it does bring it back to the sermon. Helping our children practice this discipline is fundamental. When my daughter was young and before she learned to read, I would write five different words on her paper, tell her the words and ask her to put tick marks under each word when she heard it uttered in the sermon. She would then add them up at the end of the service and let me know that the preacher used the name of Jesus fifty-two times. As our children entered elementary school we gave them notepads for taking notes. This helps many children. In our experience though, we found it more of a distraction than a help, so we have since asked them to sit and simply listen to the sermon. If you give your young children notebooks, think about decorating the books in exciting ways, so they find them special. Allow them to draw pictures related to the sermon. However, we want to make sure that this doesn't become doodle time. We want them actively engaged with the service itself.

## BE CONSISTENT

It will take time for your children to learn how to sit still, sing the hymns, and absorb sermons. Be consistent in your expectations during the service and over time it will be rewarded. Don't allow them to doodle one week and then expect them not to the next. If they are to stand when everyone else in the congregation stands, then always make sure they do so. Consistency leads to constancy.

## HELP THEM GET TO KNOW THE PASTOR

As a pastor, I know the old adage rings true, 'They don't care how much you know until they know how much you care.' This is true for adults in the pew and it is equally true for children. Go out of your way to encourage a relationship between your children and the pastor. Help him get to know them. This will heighten their desire to listen to his preaching. In addition, foster within your children a desire to know, respect, and love their pastor. Invite him and his family over for dinner, talk with your children about how much you appreciate him, his preaching and pastoral care, and as a family pray regularly for him. If they believe you consider him someone worth listening to, they will tend to listen as well. Parents, you remain the single greatest factor in shaping your children's attitudes towards the pastor, worship, and the local church. If you express dislike for his preaching, they will too. If you talk regularly about the benefits of his preaching and how you long to hear the sermon each week, then they will often respond in-kind.

## AVOID DISTRACTIONS

Distractions come easily enough, so we should try and avoid all we can. Many families with small children find it easier to sit near the front. This may seem counter-intuitive as many families with small children tend to sit towards the back for an easy 'get-away,' but less people in front of you means less potential distractions for little eyes. Try sitting in different places around the sanctuary and find out what works for your family. Then practice it.

Crayons, reading books, and toys can become unneeded distractions. Each parent will want to consider whether their children benefit from having such things in the service. Remember, our goal is not to train our children to be quiet and still (though that is necessary), but to participate in worship.

Thank God for friends. We want to encourage our children to seek friendships in the church, but corporate worship is not the time for them to sit and talk with friends. Teenagers especially like to sit with their peers during the service, but this too easily distracts. Blessings seem to flow from a family worshiping together in the same pew or row. It speaks volumes to our children and the rest of the congregation. Relieve some of the burden from your children and tell them that when their friends ask to sit together, they should 'blame' you for it not being an option. This allows them to say, 'no,' without some of the social embarrassment.

## Talk About It on the Way Home

The car ride home often serves as one of the greatest tools in helping our children to enjoy, engage, and reap the benefits of corporate worship. Ask them questions about the service and interact with their responses. What hymn, psalm, or song sung was their favorite that morning? Why? What did it remind them of? What was the main point of the sermon? Did the sermon stir any questions in them? What illustrations did the pastor use? What applications of the text struck them? How do we apply this sermon together as a family? Where did it challenge us and where did it encourage us? Parents can ask numerous questions on the way home. Don't miss the opportunity. This can make the difference in the seed of the Word being quickly snatched away or finding fertile soil (Mark 4). Yet, whatever you do, do not turn the car ride home into a critiquing session. Too many families fall into this error. We do not attend worship to critique or criticize; we attend to commune with the Living God by His Word and Spirit (John 4). We can disciple our children to the positive or to the negative—always remember that. We will shape their thoughts and attitudes.

## STOP WORRYING

Many parents concern themselves with what other members of the congregation think of their parenting skills or their child's behavior during the service. DON'T! We want to be gracious and understanding, but others' expectations cannot dictate our parenting. Our children need to adjust, but so do the adults. *In reality, it is adults who have to adjust the most!* Everyone needs to practice a little more tolerance on this front. If a baby fusses a little, a few papers rustle, or some items drop on the floor, it is alright. The world isn't ending, worship won't stop, and God isn't displeased. Congregations need to willingly and joyfully join in this great privilege of welcoming covenant children into corporate worship. And that takes some minor adjusting on everyone's part.

## BE WISE

Of course, we never want our children to be overly distracting. If a baby is crying, a toddler keeps talking, or an elementary school child continues to get up, then we need to take the child into the hall or foyer during the service. Hopefully, with a little comfort, talking, or discipline, a child may reenter the service. When my children were young, we routinely had to leave the sanctuary. Most of the time we reentered after a little discussion, but sometimes we listened to the service via the speakers in the hall for the benefit of everyone else. Remember to love others by practicing wisdom.

## AFFIRM YOUR CHILDREN

On the ride home affirm your children. Encourage them if they behaved well and let the children know how you enjoyed worshiping alongside of them. When younger, my children often asked after the service, 'Were we good?' They wanted the encouragement and the 'well-done,' as most of us do. This is not legalism, this is training. In the years ahead it will serve as a blessing to them and to everyone else.

## BE PATIENT WITH YOUR CHILDREN

*Be patient with your children and shower them with grace.* It takes children time to adjust and different children adjust on different time tables. Your child may come into the service and sit attentively and quietly within a few weeks or you may need to help your child with this for months or even years (as has been our case!). I say this knowing the challenge— 'Be patient!' Love them and refuse to compare them to other children in the church. The challenge can be great as you observe the family of seven children sitting perfectly still, all carrying their Bibles, nodding their heads along with the sermon, singing with full voice in praise, looking like they should have halos above their heads. Remember, God blessed you with this (these) little bundle(s) of joy! Keep bringing them into the midst of God and His people in worship. Keep placing them in the way of the means of grace, and by God's grace, in due time, they will begin to worship right alongside of you.

## BE PATIENT WITH YOURSELF

Even as you seek to practice patience with your children, so you must seek to be patient with yourself. Your children's ability to sit still or not sit still is not a universal commentary upon your parenting ability. Your children's embracing of worship or not embracing of worship does not signify you are doing things right or wrong. You cannot determine the outcome. Your job is simply to remain faithful and diligent. Be patient with yourself. Be gracious to yourself. And keep looking to your Heavenly Father, who loves you even more than you love your own children.

## CONCLUSION

Parents, I know at times it is not easy. Believe me, I know. But keep your eyes fixed above. God's grace is sufficient and we know that including our children in worship will benefit them (and us) in the long-run. The day will come when they will sit next to you in worship singing the songs, reading the Scriptures, praying the prayers and won't ask even once to go to the bathroom. Persevere; the dividends will prove worth the investment.

# 6 Wisdom for Church Leaders

Every elder board, session, consistory, pastoral staff, and leadership team should wrestle with the Scriptural, theological, and practical arguments for including children in worship. If the process stirs a conviction, then courageously (and patiently as is discussed below) lead your congregation into this beneficial practice. Don't stop at conviction, be a doer. Leaders serve the Church well when they lead out of conviction, practicing what they believe is best for the people under their care, even if it means facing a little opposition.

At the outset, we need to declare that the leadership of a local church cannot and should not attempt to dictate to parents whether or not they bring their children into the corporate worship services of the church. Their children are their children. Christian leaders lead, but they don't dictate. We desire to lay the biblical rationale and theological argument before our people, set the example, and gently shepherd them, but the Lord is lord of the conscience and we will trust His working and willing.

However, the leadership of a church will set the vision, atmosphere, and expectation for including in or excluding children from worship. And this will do much to determine its acceptance, practice, and embracement by the entire congregation. We cannot underestimate the determination of the leadership.

## SET THE EXPECTATION

Though the leadership of the church cannot and should not force parents to include their children in the corporate worship service, it must clearly state its expectations regarding normative practice for parents and their children. If the church leaves this unsaid or poorly communicated, then most parents will choose to keep their children out of the services until they reach some magical age of understanding. This tends to be the easier path and so, unfortunately, the path most often taken. In addition, without the church's leadership clearly stating its expectation it increases the likelihood that other members of the congregation will exercise less patience with a busy toddler or fussy baby. This has the added effect of discouraging parents, because they don't want to upset others in the church.

Leaders, communicate that your church welcomes children of all ages because they are members of the visible church. Regularly remind the congregation through the bulletins or announcements that this is a conscience choice, will require some patience, and at times, even a degree of tolerance. Some children will fidget, a little added background noise will exist, and the distraction of children coming and going to the bathroom may occur—all this is to be expected. Furthermore, encourage the congregation to help young parents feel comfortable with bringing their children into the service. Challenge the congregation to engage in some simple practices that will encourage the parents and their children: give a smile to a struggling Mom or Dad, get to know children sitting next to you in the pew, volunteer to help a family on Sunday mornings, relay to families the blessings you receive by seeing them worship together.

This type of leading fosters a gracious congregation with a warm-hearted affection for the children in its midst and compassion for young parents struggling on Sunday mornings. Such a vision enables a church to be more forgiving, patient, kind, loving, and nurturing. And what elder or pastor doesn't want to see this reflected in his people?

## PASTORAL SENSITIVITY

Leaders in a local church can move too suddenly when convinced of the importance of encouraging children to attend corporate worship. I was such a leader in one church I served. The church existed for fifty years before I came as one of its pastors and as far as I could tell had never included children in its services. For at least fifteen years it promoted children's church at the same hour as the corporate worship services. Children were seldom seen in the worship service. I passionately led the elders through a series of meetings in which we studied the Scriptures and the implications of this practice. They quickly grew in conviction and wanted the children of the church included in corporate worship. I then proceeded to schedule a meeting with the parents in the congregation. A handful of parents expressed concern at the first meeting, so I scheduled a second meeting. When the concerns still presented themselves, I foolishly charged ahead. We abruptly cancelled children's church, kept a nursery for three and under, and moved-on. This proved too soon for some of these families. As a pastor, I didn't help them adequately prepare for or adjust to this change, erred by acting too swiftly with change and lacked pastoral sensitivity. As leaders, we need to lead, but we must do so with care.

## Don't Be Overzealous

On a related note, leaders of the church do well not to overzealously apply their conviction. Commit to welcoming children into your worship services and clearly communicate that decision to the congregation, but know that some families will find it too difficult. As elders and pastors, we should attempt to help and encourage them, but not force it upon them by excluding all other possibilities. A wise church provides a nursery for children three or four or even five or six years and under. It allows unconvinced families not to feel coerced or like they need to leave the church. It possesses the added benefit of providing a helpful avenue for visiting families who might find this practice foreign or strange. Consider it part of your hospitality ministry and joyfully embrace tentative parents and their children by providing limited alternatives as you continue to teach them. We do the Christian family little service if, in trying to include the whole family in the central act of the life of the church, the effect is actually opening the door for the entire family to leave the church. Conviction and pastoral sensitivity make for wise and godly leadership.

## AVOID COMPETITION

No doubt, there remains value in graded approaches to Christian education. It serves a real purpose to teach second graders in a different venue from seniors in high school. In no way should we oppose Sunday school. However, we should oppose forsaking corporate worship for the purpose of attending Sunday School. They should not be in competition. The schedule itself, for example offering Sunday school at a different hour from the worship service, can serve as a gentle nudge toward the godly and helpful practice of including our children in corporate worship.

## PROVIDE HELPS

Help the children of your church throughout the week. Encourage family worship in your congregation.[1] I find the practice of family worship serves as one of the greatest helps to incorporating children into corporate worship. Train, equip, and challenge families to gather each night to read the Scriptures, pray, and sing. Create a weekly family worship guide for families to follow. The Bible readings or hymns/songs could tie into the service for the upcoming Sunday or the past Sunday. In this way, you help children to prepare for what they will hear or digest what they already heard. Connect the subjects

---

1. I have written a book on this topic, *A Neglected Grace: Family Worship in the Christian Home.*

they learn in Sunday school with the sermon series in corporate worship. Sing a hymn of the month in your services so children learn some of the songs of the faith and can sound forth with a full voice. Brainstorm with your leadership and parents how to help children connect more with the services. Their good ideas may just surprise you!

## INTRODUCTION TO WORSHIP

I encourage churches to annually or bi-annually conduct an 'Introduction to Worship' class for parents and children. Walk through the different elements in the worship service. Help parents and children understand and value what occurs in worship. Many treat it as casual, because they lack understanding of worship's significance. A poverty of knowledge breeds frustration. Boredom quickly afflicts because the purpose remains hidden. The more kids know, the more they will engage. The more they appreciate, the more they will delight in it. The more they understand, the more it will prove meaningful to them. Church leadership can also use these classes to practically equip parents with some of the suggestions found in Chapter 5 and to keep setting the vision before the entire congregation.

## GET TO KNOW CHILDREN

Pastors and elders, get to know children in your congregation. Learn their names, their likes and dislikes, their favorite classes and activities. In turn, let them get to know you. In my childhood a pastor showed special interest in me. As far as I know, he was the only pastor who ever knew my name before I reached my college years. He took time each Sunday to greet me. He loved to tease me about my being a Chicago Cubs fan (which provides a lot of fodder for teasing!). When he entered the pulpit, I listened. Why? Because he knew me and I felt like I knew him. As is often the case in life, I considered him someone worth listening to, because he considered me.

I know another pastor who carries around a pocket full of candy. The children in the church approach him after the service if they memorized a new Bible verse. I have watched this scene play out on numerous occasions. He makes it quite purposeful. When a child approaches him, he stops, looks them in the eye, and asks if they memorized a new verse. When they reply, 'Yes,' he takes them to a set of chairs in the room and sits down across from them. Then, he patiently listens as they articulate the new memorized verse. If they recite it correctly, he pulls a handful of candy out of his pocket and the child picks any piece they like. Do you think those children believe this pastor cares for them? Without a doubt!

Children are part of your flock. Get to know them. Let them get to know you. It will drastically affect your preaching and teaching ministry to them. They will be much more attentive to the voice of the Great Shepherd as He speaks through you, if you take the time to speak to them.

## CONSIDER CHILDREN WHEN PREACHING

As a preacher, we desire to reach all those who sit under our preaching. It is seldom possible to affect every person in every life-situation with one sermon. Yet, over the course of weeks our sermons should touch various types

71

of people from the lost to the faithful, from the skeptic to the over-confident, from the struggling sinner to the tired saint. We seek to speak into the lives of mothers, fathers, husbands, wives, and children. Yes, children! If children attend our worship services, then our sermons must seek to address them over time. Use illustrations that pique their curiosity. I have often watched children become more focused when the preacher gives an illustration from his childhood. It connects with them. Do not be shy about speaking directly to them at points in the sermon or in application. I love hearing pastors say, 'Children, I want you to hear what I am about to tell you...' Like soldiers in the ranks, their heads perk up and they sit in a kind of salute, ready to receive. When you prepare sermons think about the adults *and* the children under your care.

## SHOW CHILDREN ARE A PRIORITY

As we mentioned earlier in this book, the Lord Jesus blessed the little children when they came to him (Matt. 19:14). As a pastor or elder, it is a good practice to regularly bless the children under our care. This can be realized in different ways. One church I regularly preach at invites families forward for the receiving of the Lord's Table. As families journey to the front of the sanctuary, they create a half-circle. The pastor begins on one side, followed by an elder, with each distributing an element of the Table. As the pastor approaches a child, who has not yet been received as a communing member, instead of extending the bread he extends his hand upon their head and prays a short prayer for them. This includes the children in the service and engages them in the life of the congregation. The ways to do this are countless: a church may regularly pray for its children in corporate worship, allow teenage or elementary age children to serve as junior ushers or greeters, highlight Sunday mornings with baptisms, celebrate covenant children becoming communing members, etc.

## DON'T BECOME PROGRAM-FOCUSED

Churches with a vibrant ministry to children often engage children with Sunday School classes, youth group, Vacation Bible School, a children's choir, or other activities within its body life. All of these ministries serve a real purpose and bless our children and families. However, when we promote these as the primary ministry to our covenant children, then we undermine the importance of corporate worship. Church leaders, do not undersell corporate worship consciously or unconsciously by the way you speak about other wonderful opportunities for children in the church.

## CONCLUSION

Pastors and elders set the tone for the church's expectations and practices. You may receive pushback from every demographic in your church—from young families scared of the prospect, to older members of the congregation concerned about the distraction. Pray through it. Take it slow. Be patient. Maintain pastoral sensitivity. But never shrink from doing the difficult thing. Having children in our worship services is well worth it. Many of those children will thank you in the years to come, if not here, in eternity.

# 7 Not so Helpful Replacements and Objections

Healthy churches think through their ministry to children. Most of us love children and see them as a gift from above (Ps. 127:5). We desire to see our children come to saving faith and grow in righteousness and holiness. Therefore, I am convinced most churches want what is best for the children in their midst. Much discussion and forethought goes into the alternatives offered to including children in worship. Yet, I would suggest that these prove unhelpful. Though the motivations are often right, the results are disastrous.

## Sunday School as a Replacement

Most of us love Sunday school. Some of our fondest moments of ministry occurred in a Sunday school classroom: laughter swirls through the air, a semi-circle of children sits on the floor listening to the Bible, a child's curiosity sparks a penetrating question, the smell of glue and the glitter of crafts fill the room. What isn't there to like?! But as much as we love Sunday school, it cannot and must not serve as a replacement for our children participating in corporate worship.

Maybe it would help to think through the history of Sunday schools. They originated due to need. In the late eighteenth century British Christians recognized the dearth of learning among the children of working class families. The Industrial Revolution had changed society and families. The frenetic pace and demand of the Revolution called to its service entire families. Children often labored alongside of their parents in the factories and coal mines, working long hours. Due to such working hours, the opportunity for education became non-existent. Most families enjoyed only one day off during the week, Sundays.

In this context the Sunday school movement was born. Compassionate Christian men and women looked upon this scene and grieved at the loss these children would experience through illiteracy. Chief among those losses would be their ability to read the Scriptures. Therefore, Christian men and women gave of their time on Sunday afternoons to teach working class children how to read the Bible. This movement spread across the United Kingdom gaining popularity. It then journeyed across the Atlantic Ocean to the United States where it took firm root and over the centuries produced bountiful fruit. However, it is helpful to realize that the Sunday school movement was born to give children an education. Its purpose was never to remove children from sitting under the Word of God, but rather to place them under it.

Sunday school changed with the advent of child-labor laws and compulsory state education. No longer could factory owners take advantage of children with long hours and low pay; instead the government required children to attend school during the week. Reading and writing became the domain of the public school system and Sunday school gradually changed. It morphed into the modern day practice of age-appropriate Bible-teaching, crafts, games, and songs. And many children have enjoyed the blessing.

Yet, it is a blessing in its right place. Dessert proves a blessing when it accompanies a good meal, but a dietary life of desserts alone affords no blessing at all. In a similar way, Sunday school blesses our children. It supports, reinforces, encourages, and engages our children with the very truths and realities they hear and see in corporate worship. When it takes the place of corporate worship, it steals these benefits and it lacks the ability to replace them. Like dessert, it provides benefits and enjoyments, but a steady diet without experiencing the richness of worship in the body of Christ will lead to malnourishment, no matter how sweet and good it tastes in the moment.

I would love for every church to provide age-appropriate Sunday school classes for the children of its congregation. That is a noble goal. We accomplish and encourage much in such a venue. But its appropriate domain is at a separate or subsequent hour to the corporate worship service instead of in competition with it. It lacks wisdom to place our children in something that proves helpful for them at the cost of removing them from something that proves great for them.

## Children's Church as Replacement

Children's church is a rather recent development. Many who practice it do so because they are reticent to place children in Sunday school classes without any 'worship experience'. They believe children's church provides a kind-of 'stop-gap' between traditional Sunday school and corporate worship. This approach is commendable in many ways. The desire to have children worshiping is good and right, as well as the desire to engage children with the truth of the Scriptures. Proponents of children's church contend that it becomes a venue for teaching the Bible in a way children understand. The service often engages children with puppet shows, movie clips, or dramas. Lively music, often accompanied by actions, dominates the service. Usually, the setting trumpets fun and the speaker radiates humor. Again, the motivations are often right, but the results are not quite as helpful.

Unfortunately, worship is turned on its head and tends to become entertainment. Instead of God being the focus, our children become the focus. And when man, no matter his or her age, becomes the focus of worship, it ceases to be worship. There is nothing wrong with children being engaged with puppets and dramas, but not as a substitute for worship. As Christian parents, pastors, and elders, we long for our children to realize that they are not the center of the universe, God is. We desire to see their lives marked not by self-seeking, but God-seeking.

We now face a generation of teenagers and young adults who struggle with corporate worship and the institutional church. The myriad of movements in recent decades to disavow the need for corporate worship or even the church itself provides the evidence. In some ways, this response should not surprise. A child raised in the church today can attend church every Sunday morning of their lives from nursery to high school and never participate in corporate worship. In its place they spend their early elementary years doing crafts and playing games, their later elementary years attending children's church filled with bright lights, jokes, and dramas, their junior and senior high years with couches, loud music, and engaging movies. They never experience the seriousness, joy, and transcendence of a holy God. When they finally enter into corporate worship as an adult, it feels non-participatory and foreign. And rightfully so! We set them up for this disillusionment by years of revolving the church and its ministry around them, instead of them around God. Children's church may not prepare them for corporate worship as much as we assume, and even more importantly, it may not prepare them for a life lived unto God as much as we hope.

## Worship Training as Replacement

Worship training serves as the best alternative to corporate worship, but it also proves insufficient. Again, the motives are usually good and right. The adults leading the program aim to include children in worship, but believe they remain too young to do so at this point. Therefore, the church institutes a worship training class in which children participate in some of the elements of corporate worship and receive teaching at their cognitive level regarding those elements. This training fills a needed void in many churches. We would all do well to have such training and education opportunities for our children, but not in place of including them in worship. No matter how good the training, it cannot compare with worship itself. A child attending worship promotes a child who actually worships. Experience proves time and again to be the greatest teacher.

We know this. When my children were two and three years old, I did not sit them down and lecture them about swimming on their cognitive level. Neither did I tell them to sit in the grass and just wait until they were older. I brought them into the pool with me. They 'swam' under my watchful care. Did they at two or three years of age know how to freestyle, backstroke, or even float? Of course not. Yet, over time and with experience they learned to swim. They became more comfortable in the water. It came by experience and as they watched their mother and me, the more experienced swimmers. Eventually, they began swimming by themselves. In the beginning they couldn't perform every aquatic exercise, but more came as they continued to grow in maturity and experience. No amount of teaching or even practicing small things in the bathtub would have made them as confident swimmers as they became by actually learning in the pool itself.

## OBJECTIONS

The objections to including children in corporate worship services vary. I cannot address them all, but I want to offer a response to the most common objections.

### Children Find Worship Boring

A common objection to children worshiping with the rest of the church is the suggestion that corporate worship bores children. No doubt, corporate worship could bore children, but we need to reject the assertion that it must bore children. As stated in the first chapter, worship is fundamentally a meeting between God and His people. God communes with us and we with Him. One may call corporate worship many things, but boring is not one of them. We, the covenant community, meet with the Living

Triune Holy God of the universe in worship. How can we ever label that as boring?

If our children find themselves bored in worship, then let us teach them the significance of the event. Let us model before them the joy of worship. Let us encourage and help them to engage in this holy other act. Let us pray that God fills them with the same delight we ourselves experience in worshiping the Sovereign God of the universe. And if we lack in that delight, then let us seek God and plead with Him to work in us, that our delight might be a means by which He sparks faith-filled interest in our children.

My daughter loves history probably because her father loves history. I can't help but talk about it with excitement. The generals, the presidents, missionaries, explorers, inventions, discoveries, tragedies, and triumphs thrill me. She loves when I tell her history stories. I read her books about history and we play imagination games depicting different events and people in history. She only knows history as exciting. Now that she is a little older, I watch as she sits down to read a book on Lewis and Clark's expedition or the Pilgrims or the ancient Egyptians. These events enthrall her. My delight filled her with delight. Our children often catch what we project.

I understand our worship services cannot compete with the hilarity of PBS cartoons, the split-second action of video games, or the constant pace of digitally enhanced movies, but we do well to encourage our children to discover the unique joy of worship. Will it always be exciting? No, but neither is every second of their school day, ballet class, or even their soccer game.

### Aren't We Just Going to Turn Our Children Away?

Many parents fear bringing their children into worship too early because it might 'turn them off' from worship or even faith in Christ. Why not wait until they reach an older age and they can make their own decision to attend? Or at least wait until they understand all the elements of corporate worship? The concern is understandable, but misplaced. Do we think our children will fall in love with worship by being kept from it? They may not like it or understand all of it, but as they grow in their knowledge of the Lord they will appreciate it more and more.

We do not use this reasoning in other realms. For example, fathers disciple their sons to love baseball by taking them to ballgames. These young boys don't understand all the intricacies of balks, intentional walks, and passed balls. Someone could argue that baseball is too boring for young boys. Taking them to such a complex game may turn them away from embracing the game later as an adult. Why not wait until they can understand it better and can purchase their own ticket to the games? Yet, every time I go to a baseball stadium, young boys fill the stands. In many cases, they love going to the game for the hotdogs and cotton candy. They do not always direct their attention to the field. But they learn to appreciate the game by being at the game--participating, sensing the enthusiasm of the crowd--and they gradually grow in their knowledge and love of the game. In due time, a son cheers right alongside his father. Yet, we possess something much better to disciple our children in than mere baseball. They won't fall in love with that which they never experience. This argument that our children will more likely embrace worshiping God if they aren't participating in the worship of God smacks of the crafty deception of our adversary. It steals children from enjoying the benefits of worship now and offers added barriers to their embracing it in the future. Meeting with God, surrounded by the worshiping community, sitting under the Word preached cannot be anything but an aid in turning our children towards God.

## Leaving with a Crying or Disobedient Child Is the Same Thing

Parents of young children will often need to leave the service with a crying or disobedient child. In an ideal world there would be no fussy or wayward children in our families, but that is not reality! If you have such a family, you are an anomaly. Count your blessings! Most of us don't know what that kind of existence would be like. This means that at times, we must, for the good of the congregation and our children, exit the room with our child in-tow. Some contend that this differs little from placing our children in Sunday school. However, that isn't the case. We *temporarily* take our children out of the service to comfort or discipline them. It is an exception, not a rule. We may lose a few moments, it may even mean the child and parent miss an entire corporate worship service, but the child does not miss every service of their youth. This simply exists as a temporary remedy for a present problem. It is right and necessary. Whereas, taking our children permanently out of worship is misguided and unnecessary.

## Parents Miss Service

The struggle is real and can cost. Parents need corporate worship and small children present a complicating factor. Their presence, at times, distracts and even inhibits worship if the parent must leave the room with a crying or disobedient child. Every parent, who has dared to bring their children into corporate worship, knows this struggle. Many parents feel as though they haven't actually experienced an uninterrupted worship service for months. But dear parents, the price paid remains worth it. Think of it as a good investment— an investment you will never regret. It is hard in the moment, but rewarding in the long-run. No doubt, it can be discouraging after months of struggle, but persevere. Keep perspective by fixing your mind on the eternal benefits and know that the wrestling in the pew will soon pass. No sacrifice we make for the sake of the Kingdom will ever leave us walking away disappointed.

## Distracts Other Adults

Our children may distract others in worship. We do well to be sensitive to this, but not overly sensitive. Even as children need to adjust to being in worship, adults need to adjust to having children in worship. In many cases, the adjustment for adults proves more difficult. We aren't used to children in our services and so they easily distract. But we are adults, we can adjust! It just may take a little effort.

I am amazed a grown man can watch television as his wife speaks to him from the kitchen and he hears nothing of what she says. Yet, if a child in the pew ahead rustles a piece of paper, he descends into the abyss of distraction. A little noise and a little activity does not need to distract. It seldom does at football games or when we watch television. As adults, we possess the ability to fight distraction and should seek to adapt for the benefit of the whole body.

Yet, if our children are *too* loud or *too* busy, then we must leave the room with them. Parents need to think about others in the church. Some parents treat too casually the distraction their children create and the entire congregation suffers. However, it has been my experience that *most* parents err on the other side of the issue. They concern themselves *too* much with their children being a disruption. The scribbling on the paper, the fussy baby, and the tapping foot sound much louder to the parent than to anyone else in the room. Our child fidgets and we tell them to stop. They fidget more and we feel like the eyes of the people behind our pew are bearing down upon us. The child continues to fidget and we begin to obsess that the entire room is fixated on our busy children. Usually, reality differs from our imaginations. Our children can be a distraction, but usually our fear of disrupting others is more of a distraction than our children have actually become.

## CONCLUSION

The replacements for and the objections to including children in corporate worship are not insignificant. Right motivations often spur the institution of replacements. Individuals offer thoughtful objections and often reluctantly. Yet, none of them rise to the level of necessitating or even encouraging our families to keep their children from corporate worship. The small victories secured in the practiced replacements and the minor difficulties expressed in the objections do not compare to the benefits and blessings our children reap by their inclusion in the worship services of God's people.

Families and churches willing to invest in their children will never regret the time or effort. The Lord reminded me of this truth earlier this year. A few families at the church I serve are related to one another. The matriarch of this extended family passed away. Though she didn't attend our church, she played such a central role in the lives of so many in our church that I decided to attend her funeral. In the service, the usual eulogies and testimonies were offered. They each remarked on her faith in Christ and that she labored to pass on that faith to her children. Her children in turn sought to pass on the faith to their children and beyond. Four generations of this family attended the funeral. The poignant moment in the service came when all her children came to the front of the sanctuary and sang the first verse of a Christian hymn in four parts. There stood her six children facing the attendees of the funeral singing praise to God in four-part harmony. As the second verse began the spouses of these children joined the song. The rich and beautiful sound filled the room. When the third verse started, my eyes filled with tears. What I thought had been rich and beautiful and full was surpassed. All of their children and grandchildren now rose and joined the hymn. Here stood five generations facing one another and singing this hymn to the glory of God. I would guess that seventy family members sang in four-part harmony that afternoon as a testimony of God's goodness and grace. It reminded me of Colossians 3:16, 'Let the word of Christ dwell in you richly, teaching and admonishing one another in all wisdom, singing psalms and hymns and spiritual songs, with thankfulness in your hearts to God.' It is good when a family worships together.

# Appendix

# Testimonials

DANIELLE SPENCER,
Lansing, Michigan—Married Mother with eight children

My husband and I have a dream that one day you could peek into our pew on a Sunday morning to see a row of eight babes singing and praying with conviction, sitting erect with Bibles open, hanging on every word of the preacher. But if you were to sit behind us next Sunday, more likely you'd find us peeling gelatinous five-year-olds off the floor, confiscating communion cup holders, and hoping that we didn't sing out loud, 'My hope is built on nothing less than, put your shoes back on!'

The endeavor to constrain elementary age children to one space to sing, pray, and listen for an hour and a half is, I'll admit, tempting to consider a fool's errand. I have certainly felt the part. Peter thought a mortal man walking on a stormy sea was a good plan until the waves started lapping at his knees. But even when he started to sink, it didn't mean he started out on the wrong adventure, only that he wasn't the hero of the story.

Because our dream has not yet been realized does not mean that we are living the wrong dream. For all the reasons mentioned in this book, we could not give our kids a better privilege than to weekly bring them into the house of God to fellowship with His people. That doesn't mean it always feels like a privilege. I saved a Sunday morning scribble sheet from my eight-year-old to remind us, 'We are utterly helpless and weak. We need a Savior that is Jesus Christ who died for sinners.' Like Peter, it is in the midst of the storm of pew problems that we have opportunity to grow in our capacity for more faith and assurance that Jesus will do all the saving – of our children and their parents!

## GINNY HALE,
Gulfport, Mississippi—Married Mom with four children

When our family joined our current church, we found it unusual in that all but the youngest children participated in the worship service. We were used to kids being segregated and entertained while the adults focused on the sermon unencumbered. We fretted about their boredom and our distraction, then sought advice from a couple with four well-behaved young worshipers.

Rather than doling out disciplinary advice or reward strategies, they introduced us to the concept of family worship. We began praying, singing and studying the Word with our children every evening. Our family grew closer, our relationship with God became deeper, and Sundays became much more joyful. Because our children had daily practice in seeking God, they were quite comfortable with being reverent, quiet and focused on the Sabbath day.

One of the greatest and most surprising benefits to spending Sunday service alongside my little ones is how they keep me on my toes. Any temptation to rehearse my grocery list rather than pay attention is quashed by their diligence. When we trace our fingers under the words in the Bible and hymnal, I pay closer attention to the text. I keep my ears open for unfamiliar words or concepts and whisper explanations to my inquisitive young ones. As Mom and Dad do, they take notes (or at least illustrate sermons) on their worship bulletins. After church we discuss the sermon, and I am usually humbled by how much they grasped or insights that I may have missed. My heart has changed as I've realized what a privilege it is to daily usher my kids into God's presence.

---

### PATRICK AND FLORY PULLIAM,
McDonough, Georgia—Married with eight children

Our eight children have always been expected to join in the worship service as soon as they are able to participate. As infants, they were left in the nursery. With our older children, at about age four they joined us for most of the service, while taking them to the nursery during the sermon, and they quickly learned how to sit through the entire service. As we added more children, we were teaching the older ones the elements of worship during family worship, and the younger ones learned right along with them, surprisingly quickly. As a result, we started bringing them to the worship service at younger ages. Because they were able to participate and to engage in worship, it was easier for them to sit still and to pay attention, even when they were two or three years old. At first, they sang the *Doxology* and the *Gloria Patri*, moving on to reciting creeds and the Lord's Prayer. Participation in worship has been made an issue of discipline when necessary, but this hasn't been much of a problem, because they seem to find such joy in joining along. When they have learned to read, we have helped them follow along with Scripture readings and singing hymns. Little ones are allowed to draw during the sermon, but not before, and they transition to a rudimentary system of taking notes (keeping tally marks, for example, for certain key words), advancing as they get older. We have taught them that we are worshiping the living God who is worthy of our worship, and that the Lord and Creator of the universe is going to speak to them through the Word that day. From very early ages, they have learned the rhythms of worship, witnessed the unity of God's people in worship, seen the sacraments, participated in worship, and have participated in that for which they were created. We have found it to be a blessing for us and encouraging to other believers to see our children worshiping with us.

---

## NATE GROELSEMA,
Grand Rapids, Michigan---Age 23, married

I am a pastor's son, which means that my time in corporate worship began at a young age. Every Sunday morning and evening I was in church, whether I liked it or not. And sometimes I really didn't. Whether I went compliantly or with complaint, my dad and mom used the opportunity to tell me that it was a privilege to gather with God's people, because so many Christians were not as privileged. It did not always make a difference, but I knew my parents genuinely regarded corporate worship as a privilege. Looking back, I realize corporate worship taught me much about God, the Bible, and my need for a personal relationship with God. Many teaching moments fueled my spiritual maturation, including the following occasion. I remember the communion plate of broken bread passing over me from my left to my mom on the right. I was confused and frustrated that I wasn't allowed to take any. My juvenile mind thought the adults were enjoying 'snack time' and excluding me, so I incompetently expressed this 'injustice' to my mom, and I did not do so quietly. It was an immature action, but it became a teaching moment, likely the reason this memory remains with me almost fifteen years later. My parents used this opportunity to explain how this Supper reminds us and causes us to celebrate Jesus' death. They expressed that one of their prayers for me was that I would join this celebration by professing my faith one day. While I can't say that I fully understood the Lord's Supper after this episode, I gained an appreciation for Christ's sacrifice and a reverence for the Lord's Table. It took years for me to consider corporate worship to be the highpoint of my week, but God's grace has brought me to this point. I have come to understand that we don't include children in church services to teach them 'church etiquette', rather, the inclusion of children is an excellent way to foster conversations about the Bible, faith, worship, and Sabbath practices with the younger generation. At the very least, this is how God worked in bringing me to Himself as a child.

## Molly Vanderwey,
Mason, Michigan—Age 14

I love attending worship at my church. Ever since I can remember, going to sit through the service with my mom and dad has not been an annoyance, but a blessing (however, I know I was fidgety sometimes!).

When I was little, corporate worship made me feel 'big'. I was just like my parents and my Sunday school teachers. I was worshiping God with them. One time I was in the service while the attendance books were being passed down the aisles. One of the other congregants, Mrs. Widder, passed the book to me. I started to pass it to my parents to sign for our family, but she stopped me and said something like, 'You are a part of this church too. You sign your name right there.' This meant the world to me.

I can't remember a specific time or experience when I first understood the gospel or wanted to profess my faith. Perhaps this is because I always heard the gospel preached as I sat in worship each week. I count this as a blessing. My pastor says it's good for kids to have boring testimonies. Often, my pastor looks out at the kids to speak specifically to us. He acknowledges us as an important part of the people he's preaching to.

Much of what I learned with respect to how to study the Bible, how to approach my sin, how to be a part of the covenant community has all been learned from worshiping with my church, and sitting under the preaching of my pastors. I am very thankful for my pastors, who have faithfully fed me gospel-filled preaching, and I am very thankful to my parents for taking me to sit through the Sunday service since I was little.

# Appendix

# B Helpful Resources

## Books on Worship

*A Better Way: Rediscovering the Drama of God-Centered Worship* (Michael Horton, Baker Books, 2002)

*Discovering the Fullness of Worship* (Paul E. Engle, Great Commission Publications, 1991)

*Give Praise to God: A Vision for Reforming Worship* (Philip Graham Ryken, Derek W.H. Thomas, and J. Ligon Duncan III, editors, P&R Publishing, 2003)

*Guides to the Reformed Tradition: Worship That Is Reformed According to Scripture* (Hughes Oliphant Old, John Knox Press, 1984)

*O Come, Let Us Worship: Corporate Worship in the Evangelical Church, Reprint Edition* (Robert G. Rayburn, Wipf & Stock Publications, 2010)

*Reformed Worship: Worship That Is According to Scripture, Revised and Expanded* (Terry L. Johnson, Reformed Academic Press, 2000)

## Books Concerning Children in Worship

*Children in the Worshipping Community* (David Ng and Virginia Thomas, John Knox Press, 1981)

*Incorporating Children in Worship* (Michelle A. Clifton-Soderstrom and David D. Bjorlin, Cascade Books, 2014)

*The Nursery of the Holy Spirit: Welcoming Children in Worship* (Daniel R. Hyde, Wipf & Stock, 2014)

*Parenting in the Pew: Guiding Your Children into the Joy of Worship* (Robbie Fox Castleman, IVP Books, 2002)

## Other Books

*A Neglected Grace: Family Worship in the Christian Home* (Jason Helopoulos, Christian Focus Publications, 2013)

*Sermon Notes for Kids Ages 6-11* (Jill Connelly, Truth Steps Publication, 2012)

*Sermon Notes for Teens* (Jill Connelly, Truth Steps Publications, 2013)

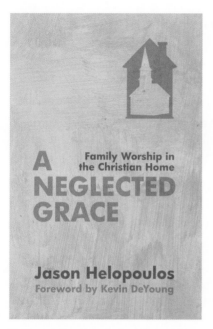

A

**Family Worship in the Christian Home**

NEGLECTED GRACE

Jason Helopoulos

Foreword by Kevin DeYoung

The author calls parents and church leaders to reclaim the practice of family worship. This indispensable means of grace directs our children to seek Christ daily, preparing them to go out into the world as fully functioning Christian adults, who love Christ and see all of life in relation to Him.

'I know firsthand that he writes as one who takes seriously all the challenges and all the opportunities fleshed out in this excellent book. The 'neglected grace' of family worship is not neglected in his home.'

Kevin DeYoung
Senior Pastor, University Reformed Church,
East Lansing, Michigan

'What we need is precisely what Pastor Jason Helopoulos has provided: a wise, realistic, gospel-motivated (rather than guilt-driven) guide that all of us can use and put into practice. I am happy to commend it, and I am eager to see how the Lord will use it for his glory and the strengthening of families!'

Justin Taylor
Executive vice president, Crossway Books
Blogger, 'Between Two Worlds', Wheaton, Illinois

ISBN 978-1-78191-203-4

# Christian Focus Publications

Our mission statement –

STAYING FAITHFUL

In dependence upon God we seek to impact the world through literature faithful to His infallible Word, the Bible. Our aim is to ensure that the Lord Jesus Christ is presented as the only hope to obtain forgiveness of sin, live a useful life and look forward to heaven with Him.

Our Books are published in four imprints:

## CHRISTIAN FOCUS

Popular works including biographies, commentaries, basic doctrine and Christian living.

## CHRISTIAN HERITAGE

Books representing some of the best material from the rich heritage of the church.

## MENTOR

Books written at a level suitable for Bible College and seminary students, pastors, and other serious readers. The imprint includes commentaries, doctrinal studies, examination of current issues and church history.

## CF4•K

Children's books for quality Bible teaching and for all age groups: Sunday school curriculum, puzzle and activity books; personal and family devotional titles, biographies and inspirational stories – because you are never too young to know Jesus!

Christian Focus Publications Ltd,
Geanies House, Fearn, Ross-shire,
IV20 1TW, Scotland, United Kingdom.
www.christianfocus.com